The Advanced Shotokan Kata Manual

Dedicated to Karate practitioners everywhere!

Mount Fuji with cherry blossom trees and a shinkansen in the foreground all three are iconic of Japan

First Published in 2009
Actikarate Ltd, 55 Shortmead Street,
Biggleswade, Beds. SG18 0AT
www.actikarate.com

Is Copyright ©2009 Actikarate Ltd

The Advanced Shōtōkan Kata Manual
Volume One. Published In Great Britain in 2009
by Actikarate Ltd

All Rights Reserved.
No part of this publication may be reproduced, stored in a retrieval system, or transmitted in any form or by any means without the prior permission in writing of the publisher, nor be otherwise circulated in any for of binding or cover other than that in which it is published and without a similar condition including this condition being imposed on the subsequent purchaser.

The views and ideas expressed in this book are solely those of the author and the people with whom they have approached. Please bear in mind that laws change, and this does not substitute the readers need to keep abreast of and/or changes in the law.
This is a training manual to be used in conjunction with tuition. It does not replace the instructor but aides the learning process. This Book is a work of non-fiction. Unless otherwise noted, the author and publisher(s) make no explicit guarantees as to the accuracy of the information contained in this book.

References and pictures have been used with copyright permission using Wikpedia, Japanese archives with no limitation to use and theoretical explanations are those of the authors using and interpreting these sources.

ISBN 978-0955727-436
Printed and Bound in Great Britain
Photography Martin Chadwick

'Karate is a life time
study reflecting in
ability, knowledge through
effort and perseverance!

It's understanding the
nature of the technique...

That's pure skill and cannot
be graded'

Acknowledgements

Frank wishes to acknowledge the following:

Azadeh, Gabriel, Michelle Ericsson, Tamer Mourssy, Reza Peyk, Judy Oliver (Local News Tv), Laura de Quincey (Reporter), Mia Matous, Sensei Stephen Mc Gregor, Tom Barrett, Gareth Hains, Matthew Harris, Joachim Grupp (Berlin), Alireza Eftikhari, Thanhtuyen Levant, Jono Lester, Warren Levi (5th Dan, Shotokan, New York, USA) Fauve Rock, my rock! Rob Miller, Rob Ho, Thierry Culliver, Christa McVoy, Diane Dobbs, Janice, Kelly & Rachael, Ataollah Mohammadi Mansour (Tehran, Iran), Peyman Niknazar Shiraz, Iran) & my father's friends.

The following supporting Karate's Olympic inclusion:

Sensei Denise Kenny, (Kyokushin Kan Karate, Canada - your special to us) Stavroula Kontostathi - for being a nice human, Bedo Karate, Stacey Lee Bolon, Chris Boulier, Frank Schneider, Paul Gibbins, Liam O'Halloran, Aarti Narotam, Alexander De Araya, Helen Crabtree, Dallas Gordon III, Martin Chapusa, Mike Farmer, Andrew Morrell. And of course lovely Ewelina Suchocka.

The Schools

Gamlingay Village College, Carlton Lower School, Harold Middle School, Thurleigh Lower School, Greenleas Lower School, Brooklands Middle School, Linslade Middle School, Everton Lower School, Everton Village Hall Committee, Dunton Lower School, Wrestlingworth Lower School. Connexions, Ofsted, John Donne Lower School.

The Team

Gazelle Book Services Ltd - Melanie & Trevor - thank you for your support in getting our message out there!

Martial Arts Illustrated Magazine - Frank's voice to the martial arts community!

Rushmoor

All of the old school friends - especially Chris Little, Derry Bass, David Ralley, Wari Pepple, Adam Ilic and Ranjit Rupra, and Imran Khan - all of the borders - and Paul Wilson - rest in peace!

Foreword

"As a competitive driver and athlete, I understand what it takes to overcome adversity and strive to reach great heights. Like Motorsport, Karate is largely misunderstood, misinterpreted and criticised by the wider public, but Frank has taken it into his power to actually *do* something about it.

His quest to have Karate accepted into the Olympics, and recognised worldwide as both a martial art, sport; and a self-defence discipline, has shown the true character of a man with the wisdom, passion, skills and perseverance to fight for what he believes in.

I admire Frank for this, and highly recommend this book as an integral part of the refining of any karateka's technique and knowledge but more importantly developing their sense of worth and ability to achieve whatever they set out to do!

Jono Lester
Professional Racing Driver
www.jonolester.com

**Actikarate Shotokan Association
Chief Instructor
Frank Nezhadpournia
5th Dan**

Student of Learning, evolving, developing!

The Advanced Shotokan Kata Manual

Preface

This is a no nonsense manual for the serious karate practitioner highlighting step by step the fundamentals to Advanced Shotokan Kata.

Frank Nezhadpournia runs a very successful Karate Association (Actikarate Ltd) he has completed in excess of 1500 workshops for victims of violence and travels a great deal internationally to teach in clubs, schools and public venues to promote Karate.

He teaches 26 classes per week having started in just one school with 8 students! This has grown into 20 schools and over 500 students with 2 more to open this year. Frank firmly believes in order to teach well you must lead well and hence he still trains in front of every student in every Dojo!

Frank has also served in the Iranian Airforce after being invited to return by Former President Hashemi Rafsanjani - and in doing so he became the first Anglo–Iranian to return. During his time there he met Azadeh and has been married to her for 15 years.

He says, *"the ultimate goal of any karateka is to develop and fight for the inclusion of Karate in everything just like Sensei Funakoshi did. I was having daily conversations with instructors from across the world.....the subject of kata kept surfacing! So it really did not take long to realise that it was time to put foot to mat and start work on it.*

If you want to know how good an instructor is. Ask them to perform Kata! Then you decide on the grade which best suits them. Everything in Karate is contained in Kata. It is the ultimate test of character.....and it is an ungraded and limitless concept!

This book is the product of my experiences and love for the art of Shotokan Karate. I have developed unique styles of training now sharing this in a factual manual for every student and instructor who wants to progress in rank, ability but more importantly in spirit!

The Advanced Shotokan Kata Manual

'According to legend Kata was invented by a Japanese master who whilst banished to an island, devised a system of putting techniques together in order to train on his own'

Contents

Bassai Dai ....

Bassai Sho ....

Jion ....

Jitte ....

Jiin ....

Hangetsu ....

Gangkaku ....

Sochin ....

Wankan ....

Chinte ....

Unsu ....

Tekki Shodan ....

Tekki Nidan ....

Tekki Sandan ....

The Advanced Shotokan Kata Manual
Okinawa

In the 14th century, when the three kingdoms on Okinawa (Chūzan, Hokuzan, and Nanzan) entered into a tributary relationship with the Ming Dynasty of China, Chinese Imperial envoys and many other Chinese arrived, some of who taught Chinese Chuan Fa (Kempo) to the Okinawans. The Okinawans combined Chinese Chuan Fa with the existing martial art of Te to form *Tō-de, Okinawan: Tū-dī*, Tang hand or China hand), sometimes called *Okinawa-te*.

In 1429, the three kingdoms on Okinawa unified to form the Kingdom of Ryūkyū. When King Shō Shin came into power in 1477, he banned the practice of martial arts. To-te and kobudo continued to be taught in secret. The ban was continued in 1609 after Okinawa was invaded by the Satsuma Domain of Japan. The bans contributed to the development of kobudo, which uses common household and farming implements as weaponry.[1][2]

By the 18th century, different types of Te had developed in three different villages - **Naha, Shuri,** and **Tomari**. The styles were named **Naha-te, Shuri-te, and Tomari-te**, respectively. Practitioners from these three villages went on to develop modern karate.

It was through Japanese society that Karate as the art of the "empty hand" gained recognition. The styles that the Okinawans brought from Te and other cultures such as Chinese boxing, Gong Fu developed as Karate, named by the Japanese.

Introduction to Kata

Karate was thought to be a very disciplined art, many styles worked on different aspects of the art: Wado Ryu ('Ryu' means school) developed a peaceful way, and spiritual development, Goju Ryu, the soft and hard way adopting many different breathing techniques and tension techniques to develop and condition the body, Shōtōkan the most traditional and direct lineage to the founding father of Karate!

Today there are many styles some developed by the Japanese and some devised by the western world. The 3 main styles recognised are:

Shōtōkan - Goju Ryu - Shito Ryu.

Through the years each style has developed Kata (Formal Exercise) to help aid the development mind, body and allow the student to practice on their own. So Kata historically helped memory retention of complex movements - back then people could not always read or write. It became a physical telling of a story. A living moving memory of the masters who created them!

Master Chojun Miyagi   Master Gichin Funakoshi   Master Kenwa Mabuni

These masters are attributed to developing their respective forms of karate. Just like 3 tributaries they organised karate into Ryu (schools) from which the above styles emerged.

The Advanced Shotokan Kata Manual

The common folk could learn something very complicated and in the process develop great physical and mental strength. Something that was only afforded to the aristocrat of the time. The Kata that are used in the 3 Ryu's, are very similar but have been modified to capture the essence of the school in which they were practiced in.

Like the Chinese concept of Chi Kung of energy cultivation karate is the general terminology for the study of this form of art, the pioneers of Okinawa and the assembly of Okinawa and Chinese arts are the founders of Kata in which modern day karate-ka (karate practitioner) practice, and unless you know what these masters wanted to achieve with Kata it will always remain a mystery. Many students where looking for spiritual development and not just to learn a primitive fighting art.

The major aspect that divides the practice of karate today and when it was developed is the social climate. Today we live in modern houses, go shopping for dinner - call the police for major problems and most of us just want a peaceful life.

Through the development of Chi kung - families worked long hours cultivating fields to grow their crops to feed themselves through the winter and prayed to gods to safe guard the family and the crops from harm.

Like Okinawan people working all day in fields who did not have the security of policing to stop other rival villages coming over and stealing their crops so they developed a system of defence using the hands and feet and farming tools to defend themselves along with their spiritual practice. This is the possible way that martial arts developed to serve the land and help cultivate health through belief and prayer into a movement like chi kung/meditation and to rest at the doorstep of the Japanese as Kata under the umbrella of karate.

Introduction to Kata

In today's climate we practice Karate for fitness, self defence or in competition. Many Chief Instructor's even in the same system make changes to Kata to reflect their own characters. To say that one school of practice is right is very narrow-minded as they all share the same conclusions. That being 'the development of the mind through physical practice.

Upholding the essence of the art through the practice of Kata in its undiluted and purest self is the ultimate goal of any club, association and organisation!' No one teacher is better than the other - some are however noticeably worse as they wonder *'off the path'* and change Kata for their own personal edification!

Remember we are learning a part of history passed down by masters of old! It is to be valued with humility, and practiced with sincerity. The 'Bow' or 'Rei' at the start and finish should mean more than just traditional gesture. Perhaps it stands for the ultimate sign of respect and something greater than ourselves.

Anko Itosu, often called the "Father of karate." Arguably the first known karate master in the world!

The Advanced Shotokan Kata Manual

After learning basic techniques comes kata, where the students develop their skills and art. Routine or basic techniques structured Okinawan masters through Chinese influence are today mainstream in all systems of karate-Do. Developed from the three Okinawan styles; Tomari, Naha, and Shuri-te.

It has been said that Master Itosu who developed the Heian katas ('Peaceful Mind forms') introduced Karate to Okinawa at the age of 77. An example of the longevity!

Each kata develops different aspects of balance, power and movement. Out of the three main branches of Karate: Kihon (Basics) Kata (Formal Exercise) and Kumite (Sparring). Out of these Kata remains the ultimate test of ability. Many enter karate for different reasons, youngsters like to spar, but this is short-lived. Without the structure of kata a practitioner holds no true ability.

Bunkai the application of applying techniques from kata develop the mental state behind forms, how to practically apply techniques and visualise your opponents.

Many techniques in kata are a mystery, and it is the bunkai that brings them alive! It is what makes this art so intriguing! Finding what works for you, Frank and Simon have seen many styles of karate and have trained with many masters. It is now their wish to provide an educational platform for the student to work with. To them not only is kata an important aspect of karate it is also a mind set like practising Tai Chi, a belief of a path which can be practiced in your seventies and even eighties!

Karate practitioners have their favourites as many do but a true test is to never neglect anyone kata as we can learn so much from all of the them, and as with anything we influence our own practice with our personality which is what brings karate to life.

Mental Preparation

It is the ultimate expression of the karate-ka - a true representation of grade and rank! If you want to know how good a black belt is - watch them perform kata! Then you decide on rank and ability! There is no cheating in Karate. If you do not put the time in you will never get really good!

It truly is like hot water - cools very quickly and takes a while to heat up. At its intensity however - you have something truly fabulous! The key is to keep it hot!

Shotokan

Gichin Funakoshi (November 10, 1868 – April 26, 1957) was the creator of Shotokan karate and is attributed as being the "father of modern karate". Following in the teachings of Anko Itosu, he was one of the Okinawan karate masters who introduced karate to the Japanese mainland in 1921

The Advanced Shotokan Kata Manual

The 'Tora no Maki'

The symbol on the right, is what is sometimes referred to as the Shotokan Tiger, is the 'tora no maki, which translates as 'tiger of the scroll (book)' or the 'tiger roll'. It is a traditional design that was drawn by the artist Hoan Kusugi (that's his signature by the tail). Thanks to its use on Funakoshi's most widely available and authoritative work, it has become the symbol used by many Shotokan and Shotokai groups across the world.

The artist, Hoan Kusugi, didn't just have this tora no maki as his claim to fame. He was also one of Funakoshi's early karate students, and was one of the people who convinced Funakoshi to stay in Japan and to continue introducing the Okinawan fighting art to the mainland.

Shoto has the meaning of 'the sound of the wind through pine trees' or 'pine waves', and was the pen-name Gichin Funakoshi used when writing his poetry. Kan means building, and the Shotokan was the name of Sensei Funakoshi's Dojo where he taught karate in Tokyo. The building was destroyed by fire in a bombing raid during WWII, but the name was used by some of Funakoshi's students when his teachings were synthesised into a uniform style (other students used the name Shotokai, and this became a slightly different style, though also directly from Funakoshi's karate).

Interestingly, sho can also be pronounced matsu, and one of the forefathers of Shotokan (among other styles) was the great Sokon Matsumura ('pine village'), a teacher of Itosu, of whom Funakoshi was a student.

Mental Preparation

The Tora no Maki

This Tora no Maki, or the Shotokan Tiger, as it is commonly called, has become the symbol of Shotokan Karate

'KATA NO JU TAIYOSO'

1. YOI NO KISIN - the concept of readiness - run through the Kata in your mind, thinking about what it represents!

2. INYO - visualising every attack and defence prior to commencement!

3. CHIKARA NO KYOJAKU - Controlling what degree of power you use for each stance.

4. WAZA NO KANKYU - think about your stances and the speed to move for each technique.

5. TAI NO SHINSUKU - the body contracting and expanding to perform each movement.6. KOKYU - Breath control Linked to the speed and movement of the technique.

7. TYAKUGAN - What are you doing? Keep an open mind!

8. KIAI - To demonstrate spirit and create power and release it at sets points

9. KEITAI NO HOJI - Correct positioning - what stance should you be in!

10. ZANSHIN - always remain on guard and imagine it is a real fight.

Bassai Dai
'To Storm a fortress (Major)

抜塞大

Name of Kata	'To Storm a Fortress'
Stances (Dachi)	Kiba - Zenkutsu - Kokutsu - Kosa - Heisoku
Connections	2 forms; Dai - Major Sho - Minor
Number of Movements	42 Movements
Synopsis	This form is at least 400 years old (based on a carbon tested, silk drawing of the form), and is a family form (Passai is the name of a family in Okinawa).
Relevant Facts	The creator was left-handed. If you keep that in mind, some of the hidden techniques will become visible!

A castle in Okinawa, storming a fortress was hard work!

The Advanced Shotokan Kata Manual

Visualising - Preparing - Get Ready

Musubi Dachi

Shizentai

Technique 1

Bassai - Dai Yoi

Technique 4

Chudan Uchi Uke
Gyaku Hanmi

The opening techniques are fast & explosive with a shift in 3 directions within seconds!

Technique 5

Chudan Soto Ude Uke
gyaku hanmi

Movements 1 & 2

GRABBING

KNEE KICK

STRIKING!

Bassai Dai

Technique 2

Hidari Chudan
Uchi Ude Uke

Technique 3

Hidari Chudan
Uchi Uke

Technique 6

Migi Chudan Soto
Ude Uke

Technique 7

Migi Chudan
Soto Uke

Movements 3 & 4

BLOCKING THE PUNCH

BREAKING THE ARM

The Advanced Shotokan Kata Manual

Technique 8

Migi Chudan Uchi Uke - Gyaku Hanmi

Slow techniques performed extremely slow paying attention to breathing!

Technique 9

Koshi Gamae

Technique 12

Chudan Zuki

Bassai Dai is a 2nd Kyu grade Kata But very hard to teach!

Technique 13

Migi Chudan Soto Uke

Movements 12 & 13

BLOCKING   PUNCHING   STRIKING

Bassai Dai

Technique 9
Chudan Tate Shuto Uke

Technique 10
Chudan Zuki

Technique 11
Chudan Soto Uchi Uke

Technique 14
Migi Chudan Shuto Uke

Technique 15
Hidari Shuto Uke

Technique 16
Migi Shuto Uke

Movements 9 & 10

BLOCKING

PUNCHING

The Advanced Shotokan Kata Manual

Technique 17	Technique 18	Technique 19

Stepping Back	Hanmi Kaeshi	Hidari Migi

Technique 22	Technique 23	Technique 24

Ryowan Gamae	Morote Age Uke	Jodan Soto Ude Uke

Movement 19

BLOCKING THE PUNCH

THRUST KICK

Bassai Dai

Technique 19

Gedan Kesage

Technique 20

Migi Chudan Shuto Uke

Technique 21

Hidari Shuto Uke

Technique 25

Chudan Tetsui
Hasami Uchi

Technique 26

Hidari Nagashi Uke
Gedan Shuto Uke

Manji Gamae

The opening 9 techniques sees 5 changes in direction indicating multiple attacks from all around! Perhaps the Kata exponent is defending the castle rather than storming it! That would marry with our concept of *'Karate Ni Sente Nashi'*……..

The Advanced Shotokan Kata Manual

Technique 28

Mikazuki Geri   Gedan Bari

Technique 29

Technique 32

Gedan Bari

Technique 33

Hidare Gedan Bari

Technique 34

Migi Gedan Bari

Movements 30, 31, & 32

STRIKING TO NECK OR HEAD - ELBOW STRIKE - GROIN PUNCH

Bassai Dai

The sequence of techniques that are repeated in shotokan kata always indicated to me that you were up against a stubborn attacker rather than repeating the same technique to multiple attackers. Yama Zuki appears 3 times in succession (above). Or perhaps for training purposes it is repeated just to get better at it!

Bassai Dai

Technique 36

Yama Zuki

Technique 37

Koshi Gamae   Yama Zuki

Front

Technique 39

Sukui Uke   Nukite

Halfway

Technique 40

Migi Shuto Uchi

Movements 37 & 41

U PUNCH TO GROIN / HEAD

KNIFE HAND STRIKE

Entry Form:-
http://www.itka-karate-greatbritain.com/Entry-Form-Sept2011.pdf

Referees and Judges Form:-
http://www.itka-karate-greatbritain.com/ITKA-Referee-and-Judges-Sept2011.pdf

Kihon kata diagrams

* Kihon - also known Taikyoku Shodan

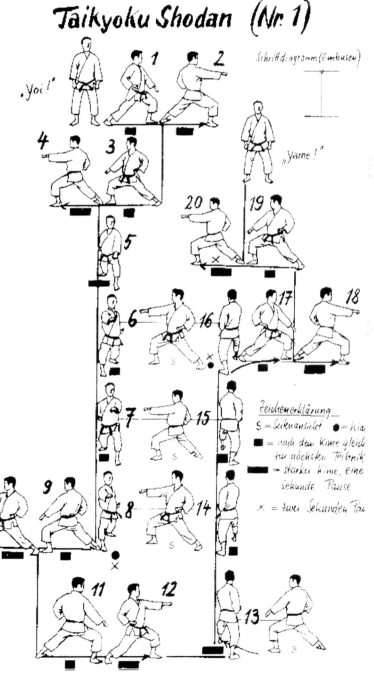

Bassai Dai

Technique 38

Gedan Uke / Sokui Uke

Technique 39

Halfway

Technique 41

Shuto Uke

Technique 42

Shuto Uke — Kiai!

Finish

Bassai Dai Yame

Movement 38

BLOCK AS A STRIKE

BOTTOM FIST STRIKE

'Kata are used in many traditional Japanese arts such as theatre like kabuki and schools of tea ceremony (chadō), but are most commonly known for their presence in the martial arts'

Pictured Left: Osakajo Castle & Tsurugajo, Aizu Wakamatsu castle.

Bassai Sho
'To Storm a fortress (minor)

抜塞小

Name of Kata	'To Storm a Fortress' (Minor)
Stances (Dachi)	Kiba - Zenkutsu - Kokutsu - Neiko Ashi
Connections	2 forms; Dai - Major Sho - Minor
Number of Movements	27 Movements
Synopsis	This form is at least 400 years old (based on a carbon tested, silk drawing of the form), and is a family form (Passai is the name of a family in Okinawa).
Relevant Facts	The creator was left-handed. If the you keep that in mind, some more of the hidden techniques will become visible!

Training in Shuri Castle, Okinawa

The Advanced Shotokan Kata Manual

Visualise

Shizentai

Technique 1

Bassai Sho Yoi — Awase Uke

Technique 4

Ushiro Gedan Tettsui Uke — Halfway — Gedan Bari

Movements 1, 2 & 3

BLOCKING — TWSITING — BREAKING

Bassai Sho

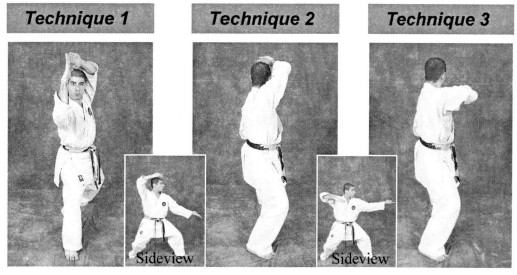

Technique 1: Jodan Awase Haisho Uke
Technique 2: Koko Uke
Technique 3: Suihei Bo - Dari

Technique 5: Bo - Dari

Technique 6: Haito Koshi Gamae

Shuto Uchi / Keage

Technique 7: Migi Tate Shuto Uke

Technique 8: Chudan Zuki

The Advanced Shotokan Kata Manual

Technique 9
Chudan Zuki

Technique 10
Manji Uke

Technique 11
Manji Uke

Technique 15
Stepping Back
Shuto Uke

Technique 16
Gyaku Hanmi
Kysho Dori

Hidari Migi
Tsukami Uke

Movements 10 & Halfway 11

DOUBLE BLOCK

TURN TO BLOCK

Bassai Sho

Technique 12 — Migi Shuto Uke
Technique 13 — Hidari Shuto Uke
Technique 14 — Migi Shuto Uke

Technique 17 — Avoid a Sweep · Gedan Kekomi
Technique 18 — Ryowan Uchi Uke

Movement 11

THE BLOCK IS AN ATTACK

The Advanced Shotokan Kata Manual

Technique 19

Jodan Heiko Ura Zuki

Technique 20

Ashi Bari / Nagashi Uke   Sokumen Morote Zuki

Technique 23

Sokumen Morote Zuki

Technique 24

HIdari Ashi Bari / Nagashi Uke   Sokumen Morote Zuki

Movements 20, Halfway & 23

SWEEP INSIDE LEG / BLOCK   STRIKING   PUNCHING THROUGH

Bassai Sho

Technique 21

Chudan Mawashi Tetsui

Technique 22 / Technique 23

Migi Oi Zuki   Ashi Bari / Nagashi Uke

Technique 25

Ashi Bari / Nagashi Uke   Sokumen Morote Zuki

Technique 26

Ura Ashigake
Shuto Doji Uke

Movement 26

STRIKING

BREAKING

The Advanced Shotokan Kata Manual

Technique 26

Haisho Uchi — Morote Hiki Otoshi

Technique 27

Ura Ashigake / Jodan Shuto Doji Uke

Technique 27

Haisho Uchi — Morote Hiki Otoshi

Finish

Bassai Sho Yame

Movement 27

STRIKING

BREAKING

Everything in Shotokan has a reason and performing a basic block such as Age Uke is no exception. The retracting arm is not just preparing to create momentum in the block, it is the block and the blocking arm can very easily be a strike!

An outside forearm block can be a strike just as the opposite arm can be a punch!

Therefore never take anything for granted! Techniques no matter how basic they may first appear are far too complicated for us to understand!

A reverse punch is also an elbow strike with the retracting opposite arm!

The Advanced Shotokan Kata Manual

HACHIKO:
A Story of Loyalty

One tale about a dog known by virtually everyone in Japan is that of Hachiko, an Akita inu. This true story is the most famous of all dog stories and has become a kind of modern legend, relayed from one generation to another and also finding its way into books, movies, and television dramas. Not only does it demonstrate the deep bond that can be formed between humans and dogs, it shows the essence of the temperament of a Japanese dog: loyalty and devotion. The legend of Hachi continues to tug at the heartstrings of Japanese people even today.

The events began roughly eighty years ago, in the early 1920s, when a certain Eisaburo Ueno, professor at the Department of Agriculture at the Imperial University (now the University of Tokyo) and resident of Shibuya, west central Tokyo, became the owner of an Akita inu puppy. The puppy came from Odate in Akita Prefecture, which was well known for producing fine Akita dogs. Born in late November (the exact date is unclear) in 1923, the puppy was delivered to Professor Ueno on January 10 the following year. Professor Ueno, who had always been a keen dog lover, named him Hachi and lavished him with love and affection.

Hachiko took to Professor Ueno extremely well, and when the professor set off to Shibuya Station in the mornings, usually at around nine A.M., either to go to the Department of Agriculture at the Imperial University or the Ministry of Agriculture and Forestry's laboratory in Nishi-gahara, Hachiko always went with him. After seeing his master off at the station, Hachiko would return home, and then in the evening at about six P.M. he would again set off to Shibuya Station and wait by the ticket gate for his master to appear. This became Hachiko's daily routine.

However, Hachiko's happy life as the pet of Professor Ueno was cut short by a very sad event, just one year and four months later. On May 21, 1925, Professor Ueno suffered a sudden stroke during a faculty meeting and died.

But it is after this that the really sad part of the story begins. After his master died, Hachiko was sent to live with relatives of Professor Ueno's who lived in Asakusa, in the eastern part of Tokyo. But he ran away repeatedly and returned to the house in Shibuya, and when a year had passed and he still hadn't taken to his new home, he was given to Professor Ueno's former gardener, who had known him since he was a puppy. But Hachiko ran away from this home repeatedly too. On realizing that his master no longer lived in the old home in Shibuya, Hachiko went every day to Shibuya Station in the same way as he always had, and waited for him to come home.

The Advanced Shotokan Kata Manual

Every day he would go and look for the figure of Professor Ueno among the returning commuters, leaving only when pangs of hunger forced him to. And he did this day after day, year in and year out. Hachiko eventually started to be noticed by people as he turned up every day at Shibuya Station.

In 1929 Hachiko contracted a severe case of mange, which nearly killed him. Due to his years spent on the street, he was thin and battle-scarred from fights with other dogs. One of his ears no longer stood up straight, and he was altogether a wretched figure, nothing like the proud, strong creature he had once been. He could have been mistaken for any old mongrel.

As Hachiko grew old, he became very weak and suffered badly from heartworms. Eventually, at the age of thirteen, in the early hours of March 8,1935, he breathed his last in a Shibuya side street. The total length of time he had waited, pining for his master, was nine years and ten months.

'Every human being is the author of his own health or disease'.

The Advanced Shotokan Kata Manual

The Teacher & Student

Teacher promises to teach, student promises to learn! Let them grow and when it's time for them to move on - wish them your best! You cannot keep a student who does not want to learn! Just as you cannot motivate one who does not want to be motivated! If Kata, Kumite, and Kihon are not enough reasons to practice karate - you are on the wrong path, and should seek another art, or sport!

Karate is hard path - it requires patience and hard work - this is a tall order for many!

'The main objective of Kata practice is to try out different combinations of techniques in a safe, practice environment to ultimately find out how to defeat your opponent'

Pictured Left: Kofukuji Temple, built 669 onwards.

Jion
'Name given from a temple'

Name of Kata	"Temple" or "Temple of love'
Stances (Dachi)	Kiba - Zenkutsu - Kokutsu
Connections	It is a representative kata in the Shotokan system because of the importance of the perfection of the basic stances in its mastery
Synopsis	Its selection by the WKF (World Karate Federation) as a shitei (compulsory) kata for Shotokan
Number of Movements	47 Movements
Relevant Facts	Jion utilises a number of stances, notably zenkutsu dachi (forward stance) and kiba dachi (horse straddle stance)

Please refer to Ten Considerations to Kata - Page 22

There are 3 essential buildings in any temple complex: a pagoda (typically three or five stories) a Great Hall (*kondō*, or *honden*), and a monastic study hall (*kōdō*?).

The Advanced Shotokan Kata Manual

Visualising - Preparing - Get Ready

Musubi Dachi

Shizentai

Technique 1

Jiai No Kamae

Technique 3

Jodan Mae Geri

Technique 4

Chudan Oi Zuki

Technique 5

Chudan Gyaku Zuki

Movement 1

A BLOCK & STRIKE

Jion

① hand down, opp of Ji'in

Technique 1

Chudan Kosa Uke

Technique 2

Chudan Kakiwake Uke

Technique 3

Halfway

Technique 6

Chudan Zuki

Technique 7

Halfway

Jodan Age Uke

Movement 7

BLOCKING

STRIKING

The Advanced Shotokan Kata Manual

Mae Geri
Technique 8

Chudan Oi Zuki
Technique 9

Gyaku Zuki
Technique 10

Chudan Gyaku Zuki
Technique 13

Halfway
Technique 14

Jodan Age Uke

Movements 14 & 16

ATTACKING

TWO TECHNIQUES IN ONE

Jion

Technique 11

Chudan Zuki

Technique 12

Halfway

Jodan Age Uke

Technique 15

Chudan Gyaku Zuki

Technique 16

Halfway

Jodan Age Uke

Movements 14 & 16

OPEN HAND BLOCK

STEPPING STRIKE

The Advanced Shotokan Kata Manual

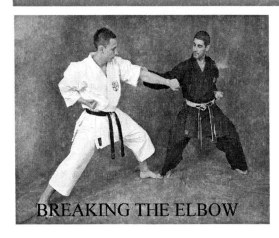

BREAKING THE ELBOW

STRIKING THE NECK

Jion

Technique 20 — Manji Uke
Technique 21 — Chudan kage Zuki
Technique 22 — Halfway
Technique 24 — Teisho Uke
Technique 25 — Halfway / Teisho Uchi
Technique 26 — Manji Uke

Movement 25 — USING THE FOREARM

The Advanced Shotokan Kata Manual

Technique 27

Jodan Morote Uchi

Technique 28

Manji Uke

Technique 29

Jodan Morote Uchi

Technique 33

Sowan Uchi Uke

Technique 34

Jodan Juji Uke

Technique 35

Ura Zuki / Age Uke

Movements 34 & 35

BLOCKING X BLOCK

STRIKING TO THE NOSE

Jion

Technique 30

Ryowan Gamae

Technique 31

Juji Uke

Technique 32

Ryowan Gamae

Technique 36

Halfway

Technique 37

Ura Zuki

Technique 38

Chudan Uchi Uke

Movements 36 & 37

PUNCHING

HOOK PUNCH

The Advanced Shotokan Kata Manual

Technique 39 — Chudan Oi Zuki
Technique 40 — Chudan Uchi Uke
Technique 41 — Chudan Oi Zuki
Technique 45 — Otoshi Uchi /Fumikomi
Technique 46 — Yumi Zuki
Technique 47 — Yumi Zuki — Kiai!

Movement 46

PUNCHING TO THE RIBS

OR PUNCHING TO FACE

Jion

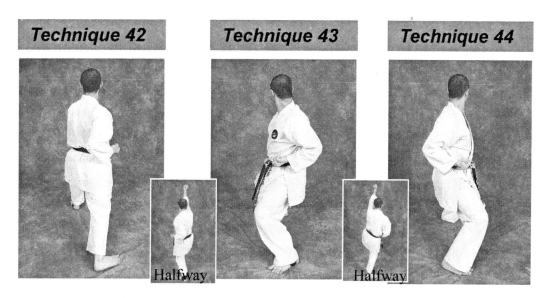

Gedan Bari   Otoshi Uchi /Fumikomi   Otoshi Uchi /Fumikomi

Jiai No Kamae

The starting and finishing position for Jion typically signifying that fighting is a last resort to a problem.

Hence the age old saying; *'I could Fight (the clenched Fist)* **but I would rather not'** (the open palm covering the fist).

But also another practical meaning for this position. Such as **'The mind under control'**. Since Karate is all about self control!

Note: This position is also repeated for Jitte and Jiin.

'Take a good look at yourself..All truths are within you... To look for truth outside yourself is to search for water outside of the ocean'

Pictured Left: Old print of Samurai warrior 'Jutte' - the power of ten hands.

Jitte
'Ten hands / ten opponents'   十 手

Name of Kata	'Ten Hands or Ten Opponents'
Stances (Dachi)	Kiba - Zenkutsu - Kokutsu
Connections	This Kata like many holds its origins from Chinese forms that had been practiced and adopted by the Okinawan masters of Te.
Synopsis	Originally called Jutte and pronounced Jite this form had been practised by the Tomari-Te masters and with its unique yama uke (hook punch) is dissimilar to other forms.
Number of Movements	24 Movements
Relevant Facts	There are believed to be many grappling techniques as well as stick attacks/defences in this kata as many arts used weapons through the ages. This is a powerful kata and although a few balancing techniques exist this arrangement expresses power and focus.

Please refer to Ten Considerations to Kata - Page 22

The Advanced Shotokan Kata Manual

Visualising - Preparing - Get Ready

Yoi

Jiai No Kamae

Technique 1

Osai Uke

Technique 2

Teisho Uke

Technique 3

Haito Uke

Halfway

Movement 1

OPEN HAND BLOCK

OPEN HAND BLOCK

Jitte

Technique 1

Osai Uke   Kake Uchi

Technique 2

Halfway

Technique 4

Haito Uchi

Technique 5

Halfway   Teisho Uke

Movements 1, 2, 3 & 4

TEMPLE STRIKE   ARM LOCK / THROAT STRIKE

The Advanced Shotokan Kata Manual

Technique 6

Teisho Uke

Technique 7

Teisho Uchi

Technique 8

Halfway

Technique 10

Halfway   Halfway   Fumikomi / Ude uke

Technique 11

Halfway

Movements 10 & 11
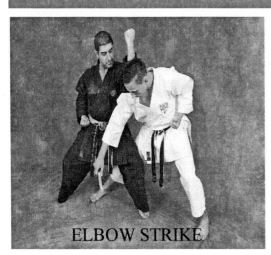
ELBOW STRIKE

SAME STRIKE

Jitte

Technique 8

Morote Gedan Bari Uke

Technique 9

Halfway   Jodan kakiwake Uke

Technique 11

Fumikomi / Ude Uke

Technique 12

Halfway   FumiKomi / Ude Uchi   Kiai!

Movement 12

LEG SWEEP OR BREAK

The Advanced Shotokan Kata Manual

Technique 13

Halfway   Ryowan Gamae

Technique 14

Halfway

Technique 16

Bo Uke

Technique 17

Jodan Bo Uke

Halfway

Movements 17

GRABBING THE ARM

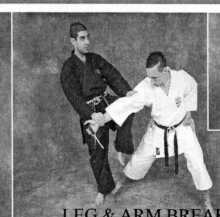
LEG & ARM BREAK

Jitte

Technique 14

Jodan Shuto Uke

Technique 15

Jodan Bo Uchi

Technique 16

Halfway

Technique 17

Bo Uke

Technique 17

Bo Uchi

Technique 18

Manji Uke

Movements 16

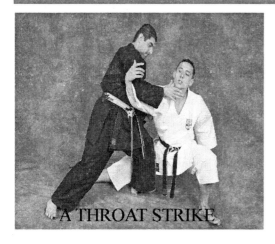
A THROAT STRIKE

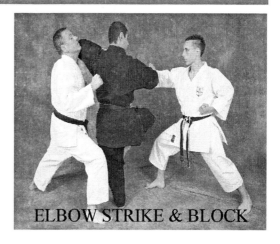
ELBOW STRIKE & BLOCK

The Advanced Shotokan Kata Manual

Technique 19	Technique 20	
Manji uke	Halfway	Jodan Age Uke

Technique 23		Technique 24
Halfway	Jodan Age Uchi	Jiai No Kamae

Movements 21

BLOCKING

DOUBLE STRIKE

Jitte

Jodan Age Uchi

Halfway

Jodan Age Uke

Jitte very aptly called 'Ten Hands' and interestingly enough lots of open hand techniques throughout the Kata as indicated here on the right.

Fighting 10 opponents shows the spirit of the Japanese and their positive nature. Study kata and you learn about the ancient Japanese way of life!

Movements 22 & 23

UPRISING STRIKE

TURNING & GRABBING

STRIKING

'To be idle is a short road to death and to be diligent is a way of life; foolish people are idle, wise people are diligent'

Pictured Left: Temple grounds maintained impeccably in Kyoto, Japan.

Jiin
'Temple Grounds'

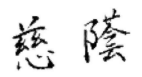

Name of Kata	'Temple grounds'
Stances (Dachi)	Kiba - Zenkutsu - Kokutsu
Connections	Was thought to have originated from the Tomari-te school of karate.
Synopsis	Sensei Funakoshi did not teach this kata extensively, and it is often neglected after black belt for its basic feel in nature! However, it remains important for the execution of many simultaneous techniques and the often repeated stances, enabling swift changes of direction while maintaining balance, power and steps of equal length
Number of Movements	35 Movements
Relevant Facts	There are rumours that it has, however, been removed from the Japan Karate Association teaching and grading syllabus. But then again there are a lot rumours flying about - the student stays true to all kata- you are in good hands! Just as in Jitte!

Please refer to Ten Considerations to Kata - Page 22

The Advanced Shotokan Kata Manual

Visualising - Preparing - Get Ready

Yoi

Jiai No Kamae

Technique 1

Chudan Kosa Uke

® hand
↓, opp
of
Jion

Technique 4

Age Uke

Technique 5

Halfway

Technique 6

Age Uke

Movement 1

DOUBLE BLOCK

Movement 2

DOUBLE STRIKE

Jiin

Temple Grounds were often surrounded by lakes

The Advanced Shotokan Kata Manual

Technique 8

Gedan Bari

Technique 9

Halfway

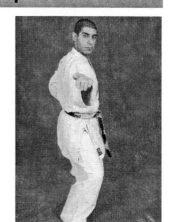

Haito Uchi

Technique 13

Jodan Mae Geri

Technique 14

Chudan Zuki

Technique 15

Chudan Gyaku Zuki

Movement 9

BLOCKING

STRIKING

Jiin

Technique 10	Technique 11	Technique 12
	 Kiai!	
Halfway	Haito Uchi	Kakewake Uke

Technique 16	Technique 17	Technique 18

Kosa Uke	Kakewake Uke	Jodan Mae Geri

Movement 10

STEPPING THRIOUGH & STRIKING

The Advanced Shotokan Kata Manual

Technique 19	Technique 20	Technique 21

Chudan Oi Zuki	Chudan Gyaku Zuki	Kosa Uke

Technique 23	Technique 24	

Tettsui Uchi	Halfway	Tettsui Uchi

Movements 19, 20 & 21

NOT EVERYTHING GOES TO PLAN

Jiin

Technique 22

Halfway　　　　Tettsui Uchi

Technique 23

Halfway

Technique 25

Halfway　　　　Tate Shuto Uke

Technique 26

Chudan Gyaku Zuki

Movements 25, 26 & 27

BLOCKING KICKS

COUNTER STRIKING

The Advanced Shotokan Kata Manual

Technique 27   **Technique 28**   **Technique 29**

Chudan Zuki   Jodan Mae Geri   Kosa Uke

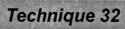   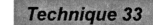

Technique 32   **Technique 33**

Halfway   Uchi Uke   Jodan Zuki

Movements 29

BLOCK BECOMES A STRIKE   BASIC BUKAI

Jiin

Technique 30

Halfway

Kosa Uke

Technique 31

Gedan Bari

Technique 34

Chudan Choku Zuki

Technique 35

Jiai No Kamae

Finish

Shizentai

Movements 33 & 34

ATTACKING MID AIR

FINISHING THE JOB

'As irrigators lead water where they want, as archers make their arrows straight, as Carpenters carve wood, the wise shape their minds'

Pictured Left: Master Kosaku Matsumora who taught Hangetsu to Funaoshi sensei! The symbol Ying / Yang - representing Hard / Soft - Goju Ryu style of karate - very prominent in Hangetsu

Hangetsu
'Half moon'

半月

Name of Kata	'Half Moon'
Stances (Dachi)	Hangetsu - Zenkutsu - Kokutsu Neiko - Ashi
Connections	It originates from the Naha-te school
Synopsis	The first part is executed slowly with strong breathing, stressing the development of the Hara. This sequence shares a strong similarity with sanchin. The second part of the kata is more dynamic in its execution, with an explosion of punches as well as mae geri (front kicks)
Number of movements	41 Movements
Relevant Facts	Due to the shared principles of expansion and contraction, Gichin Funakoshi substituted hangetsu for sanchin in the Shotokan curriculum. Mastery of this kata rests on mastery of hangetsu-dachi (half-moon stance) which is characterized by its semi-circular step movement of the back leg to the centre, and then forward. The kata consists of 41 movements. The older Okinawan version of this kata is known as Seisan

Please refer to Ten Considerations to Kata - Page 22

The Advanced Shotokan Kata Manual

Visualise

Shizentai

Technique 1

Halfway

Soto Uchi Uke

Technique 4

Chudan Gyaku Zuki

Technique 5

Halfway

Soto Uchi Uke

Movements 1, 2, 5, & 6

PUNCHING   BLOCKING   PUNCHING

Hangetsu

Technique 2

Chudan Gyaku Zuki

Technique 3

Halfway

Soto Uchi Uke

Technique 6

Chudan Gyaku Zuki

Technique 7

Ippon Ken Gamae

Technique 8

Ippon Ken Zuki

Movements 6, 7 & 8

GRABBING   DISENGAGE   DOUBLE PUNCH

The Advanced Shotokan Kata Manual

Technique 9

Halfway   Kaisho Yame Gamae   Halfway

Technique 13   Technique 14   Technique 15

Kaisho Kosa Uke   Kake Dori   Kaisho Kosa Uke

Movements 9

CROSSING ARMS   DOUBLE-STRIKE TO THROAT

Hangetsu

Technique 10: Kaisho Ryowan Gamae
Technique 11: Kaisho Kosa Uke
Technique 12: Kake Dori
Technique 16: Kake Dori
Technique 17: Chudan Uchi Uke
Technique 18: Chudan Gyaku tszuki

Movements 16, 17, 18 & 19

AGAIN DOUBLE STIRKE   COMBINATION   PERSEVERANCE PAYS

The Advanced Shotokan Kata Manual

Technique 19

Chudan Zuki

Technique 20

Chudan Uchi Uke

Technique 21

Gyaku Zuki

Technique 25

Side view

Chudan Zuki

Technique 26

Halfway

Engetsu Kaeshi

Movements 26, & 27

BLOCKING

GROIN KICK

BLOCK

Hangetsu

Technique 22
Chudan Zuki

Technique 23

Chudan Uchi Uke

Technique 24

Chudan Gyaku Zuki

Technique 26

Chudan Uraken Gamae

Technique 27

Hanmi Sashi Ashi

Mae Geri / Doji HazuShite

Movements 28, 29, & 30

SOMETIMES IT TAKES SEVERAL ATTEMPTS TO WIN THE FIGHT!

The Advanced Shotokan Kata Manual

Technique 28

Gedan Bari

Technique 29

Gyaku Zuki

Technique 30

Age Uke

Technique 33

Hanmi Sashi Ashi

Mae Geri / Doji Hazushite

Gedan Bari

Movements 32, & 33

BLOCKING

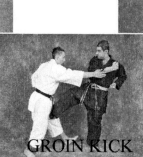
GROIN KICK

BLOCK

Hangetsu

Technique 31

Halfway

Technique 32

Engetsu Kaeshi

Technique 33

Chudan Uraken Gamae

Technique 34

Chudan Gyaku Zuki

Technique 35

Age Uke

Technique 36

Engetsu Kaeshi

Movements 34, 35, & 36

REPEATED FOR THE OTHER SIDE TO DEVELOP BALANCE

The Advanced Shotokan Kata Manual

Technique 36

Chudan Uraken Gamae

Technique 37

Kokutsu Dachi

Technique 38

Mikazuki Geri

Finish

Yame

'Kata is the ultimate test of character
There is no hiding, you are transparent!'

Movements 37, 38 & 39

BLOCKING   REVERSE COUNTER STRIKE

Hangetsu

Technique 39
Gedan Gyaku Zuki

Technique 40
Teisho Awase Gamae

Technique 41
Teisho Awase Gedan

The semi-circular movements and deep breathing promote longevity and are very indicative of the Chinese influence of Tai Chi

Hangetsu correctly performed should leave the practitioner completely exhausted.

The 'Kime' ('Dynamic Tension' of the body) especially abdomen increase muscle strength in that area! The arms, thighs and also deltoids get a heavy workout!

Some techniques have hidden applications. One thing I have learnt never take anything for granted, assume it all! Here a turn becomes a block - note the arm is in perfect position for a hook punch to the face!

*'Thousands of candles
can be lit from a single candle,
and the life of the candle will not be shortened.
Happiness never decreases by being shared'*

Chinto Kata reportedly originated in the early 19th century and named after Chinto, a Chinese sailor shipwrecked on Okinawa during a typhoon. To survive, he was forced to steal food from the local Okinawans at night. Shortly thereafter, a famous Samurai swordsman, Matsumura, was sent to capture the thief. When Matsumura finally located Chinto, an intense fight ensued, but every time Matsumura attacked, Chinto would cleverly side-step the attack and quickly counter-attack. Chinto escaped and hid in a graveyard. After falsely reporting to his lord that he had disposed of the thief, Matsumura, thoroughly impressed with the skill of Chinto, sought, found, and befriended him. He promised to keep Chinto's activities secret in exchange for instructions in Chinto's style of Chinese Boxing. Master Chinto is believed to have trained in Chuan Fa (Kempo) which was popular on China's southeastern coast. From those techniques, Matsumura formulated Chinto Kata which he taught to Chotoku Kyan - Pictured Left

Gangkaku
'Crane on the rock'

岩鶴

Name of Kata	'Crane on the Rock'
Stances (Dachi)	Kokutsu - Zenkutsu - Kiba
Connections	Coming from Chinto and modified by the Okinawan master Sokon Matsumura who studied under Master Chinto, originally this kata meant "fighter from the east" but was changed by Master Funaksohi to Gangkaku.
Synopsis	The name reflects the crane like form that is present in this kata, Its was written that through a fight Master Matsumura was equalled by this man (Chinto) who was stealing from people's crops This kata is practiced widely through many forms of karate and is a senior grade form.
Number of Movements	41 Movements
Relevant Facts	This is a difficult kata to perform with excellent balance and ankle strength required to withstand the crane stances and one footed pivots. Very seldom with karate practitioners use this kata for tournaments or gradings because of the degree of difficulty.

The Advanced Shotokan Kata Manual

Gangkaku

Technique 3 — Chudan Gyaku Zuki
Technique 4 — Gedan Bari
Technique 5 — Jodan Juji Uke
Technique 9 — Gedan Juji Uke
Technique 10 — Gedan Uke
Technique 11 — Gedan Shuto Uke
Technique 12 — Morote Shuto Uke
Technique 13 — Morote Soto Haito Uke
Technique 14 — Ryowan Gamae

The Advanced Shotokan Kata Manual

Technique 15	Technique 16	Technique 17
Manji Uke	Manji Uke	Manji Uke

Technique 21	Technique 22	Technique 23
Gamae	Mawashi Empi Uke	Mawashi Empi Uchi

Movements 21, 22 & 23

GRABBING

BREAKING

DISENGAGING

Gangkaku

There are 13 changes in direction in the performance of this kata so very difficult to keep your bearings and balance. I remember watching the Karate Kid Movie when the old and wise Miyagi sends his student out into the ocean to 'find balance' and he is practicing the 'Crane Technique' on the beach.

Somehow practicing this kata on a beach seems to serve it best - feels closer to home and you never know a crane just might drop by.......

The Advanced Shotokan Kata Manual

Technique 26

Halfway   Koshi Gamae

Technique 27

Yoko Geri Keage

Technique 30

Koshi Gamae   Uraken - Keage

Technique 31

Chudan Kage Zuki

Movements 30

HOLD YOUR GROUND   BLOCKING & STRIKING

Gangkaku

When a crane becomes aware of a distant intruding predator, or some other alarming stimulus, it adopts a characteristic posture with its head extended maximally up and somewhat forward while watching the stimulus. Typically the bird remains still, briefly. Then explodes into attack!

Now think of the kata and where that posture applies?

The Advanced Shotokan Kata Manual

Technique 34	Technique 35	Technique 36

Kage Zuki	Jodan Empi Uchi	Jodan Haito Uchi

	Technique 39	Technique 40

Rotate	Koshi Gamae	Uraken / Keage — Front

Movements 39

BLOCKING

STRIKING

Gangkaku

Technique 37

Age Empi Uchi

Technique 38

Halfway

Halfway

Halfway

Technique 41

Chudan Oi - Zuki

Finish

Yame

Movements 37 & 38

STRIKING

PULLING DOWN

The Advanced Shotokan Kata Manual

In feudal Japan the crane was protected by the ruling classes and fed by the peasants. When the feudal system was abolished in the Meiji era of the 19th century, the protection of cranes was lost. With effort they have been brought back from the brink of extinction. Japan has named one of their satellites *tsuru* (crane, the bird).

According to tradition, if one folds 1000 origami cranes one's wish for health

will be granted. Since the death of Sadako Sasaki this applies to a wish for peace as well.

As the crane approaches (or backs away from) an intruder in preparation for Attack, it will typically spread and droop its wings.

What does the bird share with this kata? Everything! Balance, change in direction, speed and slow deliberate movements ex ploding into fast ones.

The master who created this kata obviously studied his subject very well before putting this together.

Of course Chinese Kung Fu revolves around animals and mimics their movements - so why not Japanese karate too? Gangkaku does that!

Gangkaku

Above: Yoko Geri Keage strikes to the groin as opposed to the conventional kick under the arms! To the right: These blocks are turned into arm and ribs strikes!

All too often in shotokan we are programmed to associate certain techniques with certain bunkai!

Koshi Game requires excellent balance. Especially for the 180 degree spin.

There is no right or wrong in bunkai, only what works for you.

Intermediate movements are often neglected in place of the technique being performed! Top of the page: movement acts as strike!

This Open Hand intermediate movement blocks the first attacker!

To our right: The block becomes a strike!

'There is no Ushiro Mawashi Geri in any traditional Shotokan Kata! Why? Was it an unrealistic counter-attack for Bunkai? Or did it not exist as a technique yet?'

'You will not be punished for your anger, you will be punished by your anger'

Pictured Left: The famous photo of the unknown man stopping tanks at Beijing's Tiananmen Square on June 5, 1989. That's my image of immovable in the face of danger.

Sochin
'Immovable in the face of danger'

壯鎮

Name of Kata	'Immovable in the face of danger'
Stances (Dachi)	Kokutsu - Fuda Dachi
Connections	It may have derived from dragon style, and was taught in the Naha-te school in Okinawa by Seisho Aragaki. It was then passed down to Shito-ryu. Later, a variation of it was introduced into Shotokan by Gichin Funakoshi's son, Yoshitaka.
Synopsis	The rhythm of the kata is dynamic, it is characterized by slow, deliberate movements interspersed with explosive out-bursts of speed. In the Shotokan version, the powerful dominant stance in this kata is *sochin-dachi* ("rooted stance"). said to develop Chi energy.
Number of Movements	43 Movements
Relevant Facts	Rhythm is important in the execution of this kata. This kata has been said to develop Chi energy.

Please refer to Ten Considerations to Kata - Page 22

The Advanced Shotokan Kata Mnual

Visualise

Shizentai

Technique 1

Halfway   Gedan Uke / Age Uke

Technique 4

Chudan Gyaku Zuki

Technique 5

Halfway   Manji Uke

Movements 1 & 2

DOUBLE BLOCKING   BLOCK & STRIKE

Sochin

Technique 2

Halfway

Chudan Tate Shuto Uke

Technique 3

Chudan Zuki

Technique 6

Halfway

Gedan Uke / Age Uke

Technique 7

Halfway

Movements 2, 3 & 4

BLOCKING   STRIKING

The Advanced Shotokan Kata Manual

Technique 7

Chudan Tate Shuto Uke

Technique 8

Chudan Zuki

Technique 9

Chudan Gyaku Zuki

Technique 12

Halfway

Chudan Tate Shuto Uke

Technique 13

Chudan Zuki

Technique 17

Mawashi Emp Uchi

'Kata has to stand for something greater than ourselves a piece of perfection!'

Technique 18

Hikite Gamae

Sochin

Technique 10

Manji Uke

Technique 11

Halfway

Gedan Bari / Age Uke

Technique 14

Chudan Gyaku Zuki

Technique 15

Hikite Gamae

Technique 16

Uraken / Yoko Geri

Technique 19

Uraken Uke

Technique 20

Yoko Geri Keage

Technique 21
Mawashi Empi uchi

The Advanced Shotokan Kata Manual

A SERIES OF COUNTER ATTACKS AGAINST THE SAME TARGET

Sochin

The Advanced Shotokan Kata Manual

Technique 34 — Halfway — Gedan Bari / Age Uke

Technique 35 — Halfway — Soto Uchi uke

Technique 39 — Halfway — Chudan Uchi Uke — Halfway — Gyaku Uchi uke

Technique 40 — Jodan Mae Geri

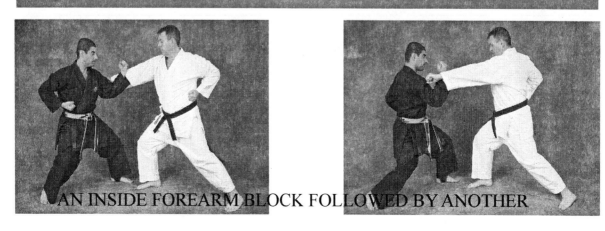

Movements 39 & 40

AN INSIDE FOREARM BLOCK FOLLOWED BY ANOTHER

Sochin

Technique 36 — Chudan Oi Zuki (Halfway)
Technique 37 — Soto Uchi Uke
Technique 38 — Chudan Oi Zuki
Technique 41 — Yumi Zuki
Technique 42 — Chudan Gyaku Zuki
Technique 43 — Chudan Zuki — Kiai!

Movements 41, 42 & 43

FRONT KICK AND DOUBLE PUNCH FINISH OFF THE ATTACKER!

'Without health life is not life; it is only a state of languor and suffering an image of death'

Pictures Left: The Crown and a humble stance - seldom can pride and humility be found together.

Wankan
'King's crown'

Name of Kata	'King's Crown' or 'Emperor's Crown' (also called **Okan**)
Stances (Dachi)	Neiko Ashi - Zenkutsu - Fuda
Connections	Not much is known about the history of this kata. It originates from the Tomari-te school and in modern karate is practiced in Shorin-ryu, Shotokan, Genseiryu and Matsubayashi-ryu.
Synopsis	It is often considered an advanced kata, despite its brevity. Karate master Shoshin Nagamine considered *wankan* to be his favorite kata. A quote from his book describes the kata as "being characterized by unitary sequences of attack and defence
Number of Movements	25 Movements
Relevant Facts	Makite Uke (Winding Knife Hand Block) and Sayu Zuki (Side punch) are introduced in this kata. (In Shorin-Ryu and Matsubayashi-Ryu)

Please refer to Ten Considerations to Kata -

The Advanced Shotokan Kata Manual

Technique 1

Turn the Head - Start Moving - Neiko Ashi Dachi

Kakewake Uke

Technique 4

Jodan Hasami Uke

Technique 5

Zenkutsu Dachi

Technique 6

Halfway

Movements 4 & 5

BLOCKING

KNEE KICK

EARLY STRIKE

Wankan

Technique 2

Turn the Head

Neiko Ashi Dachi

Technique 3

Kakewake Uke

Technique 6

Gyaku Tate Shuto Uke

Technique 7

Chudan Zuki

Technique 8

Chudan Gyaku Zuki

Movements 6, 7 & 8

PUSHING AWAY   PUNCHING   KNOCKOUT PUNCH

The Advanced Shotokan Kata Manual

Technique 9

Halfway   Hidari Gedan- Koko-Sukui-Uke   Halfway
         Migi Gedan-Koko- Zuki- Dashi

Technique 13

Technique 14

Halfway   Hidari Gedan- Koko-Sukui-Uke   Halfway
         Migi Gedan-Koko- Zuki- Dashi

Movements 9

BLOCKING AND ATTACKING   BLOCKING AND BREAKING

Wankan

Technique 10	Technique 11	Technique 12

Gyaku Tate Shuto Uke	Gyaku Zuki	Chudan Zuki

Technique 14	Technique 15	Technique 16

Gyaku Tate Shuto Uke	Gyaku Zuki	Chudan Zuki

Technique 17	Technique 18	

Yoko Kensui Uchi	Halfway	Jodan Mae Geri

The Advanced Shotokan Kata Manual

Technique 19

Chudan Oi Zuki

Technique 20

Jodan Mae Geri

Technique 21

Chudan Oi Zuki

Technique 25 / Finish

Yama Zuki   Yame

Movements 21 & 22

PUNCH BECOMES A CUT

LEAN AND KICK

Wankan

Jodan Mae Geri

Chudan Oi Zuki

Ryowan Gamae

Movements 24 & 25

GRABBING THE HEAD

PULLING THE HEAD DOWN

ROTATING THE BODY

CONTINUE THE CYCLE

'To enjoy good health, to bring true happiness to one's family, to bring peace to all, one must first discipline and control one's own mind. If a man can control his mind he can find the way to Enlightenment, and all wisdom and virtue will naturally come to him'

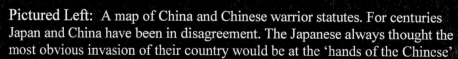

Pictured Left: A map of China and Chinese warrior statutes. For centuries Japan and China have been in disagreement. The Japanese always thought the most obvious invasion of their country would be at the 'hands of the Chinese'

Chinte
'Chinese hands or strange hands'

Name of Kata	'Chinese hands' or 'Strange hands'
Stances (Dachi)	Heisoku - Zenkutsu - Fuda Kokutsu - Kiba
Connections	The word 'Chinte' means rare hand or china hand, Master Funakoshi the founder of shotokan renamed this kata Shoin. Because of the strange techniques and circular techniques like in Bagua (Chinese arts)
Synopsis	The practice of this kata expresses circular arm movements balance and different hand attacks. This is an unusual kata but develops many good qualities like tradition and custom.
Number of Movements	34 Movements
Relevant Facts	Chinte today in most organisations is made an association kata - meaning it does not have to be learned for any examination but everyone should know it! Perhaps the greatest gift to us is examining ourselves through Kata!

Please refer to Ten Considerations to Kata - Page 22

The Advanced Shotokan Kata Manual

Visualise

Chinte Yoi

Technique 1

Halfway

Tettsui Uchi

Technique 4

Turn Head

Awase Shuto Uke

Technique 5

Tate Shuto Uke

Movements 1 & 3

BLOCKING

ELBOW STRIKE

GRABBING

Chinte

Technique 2 — Gamae
Technique 3 — Halfway / Tettsui Uchi
Technique 6 — Tate Ken Gyaku Zuki (Side view)
Technique 7 — Halfway / Tate Shuto Uke
Technique 8 — Tate Ken Gyaku Zuki (Side view)

Movements 4, 5 & 6
BLOCKING — ELBOW STRIKE — GRABBING

The Advanced Shotokan Kata Manual

Tate Shuto Uke   Tate Empi Uchi   Shuto Uke

Gedan Tettsui Uchi   Morote Enshin Haito Bari   Ryowan Uchi Uke

Variations to Movements 14

BLOCKING   ROTATING   BLOCKING

Chinte

Technique 12

Shuto Uke

Technique 13

Mae Geri

Technique 14

Naiwan Sukui Nage

Halfway

Technique 17

Ryowan Gamae

Technique 18

Ippon Ken Furi

Movements 18, & 19

BLOCKING

STRIKING THE CHEST

STRIKING THE NOSE

The Advanced Shotokan Kata Manual

Technique 19

Ippon Ken Gyaku
Furi Otoshi

Halfway

Technique 20

Chudan Nihon Uke

Technique 21

Nihon Uchi

Technique 25

Teisho Uchi

Front

Technique 26

Haiman Hasami Uchi

Technique 27

Kiai!

Chudan Hasami Zuki

Technique 31

Tate Zuki

Technique 32

Tsutsumi Ken

Jump

Chinte

Technique 22	Technique 23	Technique 24
Nihon Uke	Nihon Uchi	Teisho Furi Uchi

Technique 28	Technique 29	Technique 30
Tate Shuto Uke	Tate Ken Gyaku Zuki	Tate Shuto Uke

Tsutsumi Ken

Technique 33 — Jump

Technique 34 — Tsutsumi Ken

The Advanced Shotokan Kata Manual

Technique 34

Jump   Tsutsumi Ken

Finish

Yame

Movements 32, 33 & 34

JUMP & AVOID

JUMP & AVOID

JUMP & PREPARE

STAMPING & BREAKING

Karate means nothing if it cannot be shared!

Top Left: Training in Kerman, Iran
Top Right: Training in Berlin with Sensei Dirk Zimmerman
Bottom Picture: The team in Berlin, Germany - we met for the first time but strange seemed we knew each other our lifetimes!

'We are formed and moulded by our thoughts. Those whose minds are shaped by selfless thoughts give joy when they speak or act. Joy follows them like a shadow that never leaves them'

The supreme water spirit Ocean covers the earth with clouds; the rain in each place is different, but the spirit has no thought of distinction. Likewise, Buddha, sovereign of truth, extends clouds of great compassion in all directions, raining differently for each practitioner, yet without discriminating among them - Unsu is a very spiritual kata performed for the more senior ranks in shotokan. Clearing the mind of thought is the ultimate goal.

Unsu
'Hands in the clouds'

雲手

Name of Kata	'Cloud hands' Shotokan practitioners name it 'Hands in the cloud' because of the opening move!
Stances (Dachi)	Zenkutsu - Kiba - Heisoku
Connections	Found in Shotokan and Shito-Ryu karate styles. The origin of Unsu is unknown, but it is of the *Dragon* style. It is somewhat a condensation of Bassai, Kanku, Jion, Empi, Jitte and Gankaku, hence it is essential to have mastered these before Unsu.
Synopsis	It contains many intricate hand techniques, such as the ippon nukite (one finger strike) in the opening sequence. Unsu also contains a spectacular 360 degree spinning double kick with a double leg take down at the same time landing on the floor before continuing. Being among the most advanced kata.
Number of Movements	48 Movements
Relevant Facts	The practice of Unsu is particularly satisfying, due to its rhythm, accent on speed, abrupt stops and numerous techniques not found in any other kata. It consists of 48 moves.

Please refer to Ten Considerations to Kata - Page 22

The Advanced Shotokan Kata Manual

Visualise	Technique 1	

Yoi	Heisoku Dachi	Unsu Yoi

Technique 3	Technique 4	Technique 5

Tate Shuto Uke Nagashi	Chudan Keito Uke	Ippon Nukite

Movements 2 & 3

BLOCKING

GRAB

PUSHING ASIDE

Unsu

Technique 2

Teisho Uke

Technique 3

Tate Shuto Uke

Technique 5

Keito Uke

Technique 6

Stepping Forward

Ippon Nukite

Movements 4 & 5 + Alternative

KEEP CONTACT

STRIKING THE THROAT

OR THE GROIN

The Advanced Shotokan Kata Manual

Technique 7

Stepping Forward   Ippon Nukite   Keito Uke

Technique 9   Technique 10

Gyaku Zuki   Tate Shuto Uke   Gyaku Zuki

Movements 8 & 9

BLOCKING   PUNCHING   BLOCKING   AND AGAIN

Unsu

Technique 8

Tate Shuto Uke   Gyaku Zuki

Technique 9

Tate Shuto Uke

Technique 11

Tate Shuto Uke   Gyaku Zuki

Technique 12

Preparation Stance

Movements 12 & 13

KICKING TO THE GROIN   &   KICKING TO THE RIBS

The Advanced Shotokan Kata Manual

Technique 12

Mawashi Geri

Technique 13

Preparation Stance · Mawashi Geri

Technique 16

Keito / Teisho Uke

Technique 17

Keito / Teisho Uke

Movements 14, 15 & 16

DOUBLE BLOCK

STRIKE AND BLOCK

Unsu

Technique 14

Tate Shuto Uke Nagashi

Technique 15

Halfway

Technique 18

Jodan Haito Uchi

Technique 19

Jodan Mae Geri

Technique 20

Ippon Dachi Soto Uke

Movements 17, 18 & 19
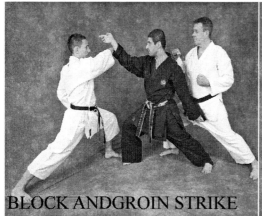
BLOCK AND GROIN STRIKE

STRIKE TO THE HEAD | GROIN KICK

The Advanced Shotokan Kata Manual

Technique 21

Gyaku Zuki

Technique 22

Jodan haito Uchi

Technique 23

Jodan Mae Geri

Technique 26

Heisoku Dachi

Technique 27

Finte 1

Finte 2

Technique 31

Tate Haito Shuto Uke

Technique 32

Halfway

Unsu

Technique 24

Ippon Dachi Soto Uke

Technique 25

Gyaku Zuki

Technique 26

Heisoku Dachi

Technique 28

Gedan Jun Zuki

Technique 29

Gedan Jun Zuki

Technique 30

Gedan Jun Zuki

Movements 27 & 28

BLOCKING

AND AGAIN

STRIKING

The Advanced Shotokan Kata Manual

Technique 32

Chudan Teisho hasami Uke

Technique 33

Chudan Mae Geri

Technique 34

Gyaku Zuki

Technique 36

Turn the head

Prepare

Jodan Haito Uke

Movements 35, 36 & 37

BLOCK   TURN & BLOCK   ROTATE & STRIKE

Unsu

Technique 34

Oi Zuki

Technique 35

Halfway

Gedan Barai

Technique 37

Halfway

Shuto Gedan Bari

Turn Head / Cross

Movements 38, 39 & 40

TURN & BLOCK   PUNCH   ROTATE & BLOCK

The Advanced Shotokan Kata Manual

Technique 38

Jodan Haito Uke

Technique 39

Kage Zuki

Technique 40

Halfway

Technique 41

Ushiro TobiGeri

Technique 42

Open Palm Hand Landing

Technique 43

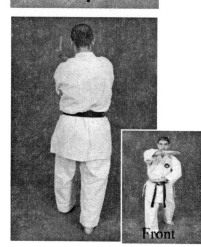

Circular Movement

Movements 41

JUMPING ROUNDHOUSE KICK

ROTATING & RETRACTING

Unsu

Technique 40

Chudan Tate Shuto

Technique 41

MIkazuki Geri & spinning 360 degrees

Technique 43

Hikite Gamae

Technique 44

Mawashi Kake Uke

Technique 45

Circular Movement

Movements 42

REVERSE KICK MID AIR

LANDING

The Advanced Shotokan Kata Manual

Technique 45

Hikite Gamae

Technique 46

Mawashi Kake Uke

Point

'Was Unsu created by a master who was left footed? Note almost all movements forward start with the left leg.

Technique 48

Jodan Mawashi Juji Uke   Gedan Ryowan Gamae

Finish
Yame

Unsu is one of the most advanced Shotokan kata, and is fairly challenging to perform. It was probably not a kata that was known to Funakoshi, and was not included in Funakoshi's "Karate-do Kyohan". It is more likely that Sense Nakayama introduced it to Shotokan later

RIGHT: One of the hardest techniques in the Kata, often neglected in tournaments.

Technique 46	Technique 47	

Turn Halfway	Jodan Age Uke	Chudan Gyaku Zuki

A number of small variations have developed since senior instructors started to break off from the JKA, the most notable being the variations in the "launch stance" (technique 40) prior to the jump. The JKA originally started from fudo dachi, with Kanazawa preferring to use kokutsu dachi. The penultimate technique (age uke) is also sometimes seen in fudo dachi, and sometimes in zenkutsu dachi.

There are also plenty of intricate movements throughout the kata

where the defender has to block and counter very quickly to move to the next attacker!

'Let us rise up and be thankful, for if we didn't learn a lot today, at least we learned a little, and if we didn't learn a little, at least we didn't get sick, and if we got sick, at least we didn't die; so let us all be thankful'

Pictured Left: Samurai warriors on horseback. Archery from the saddle was a Japanese specialty.

Tekki Shodan

鉄騎初段

Name of Kata	'Iron Horse or Iron Knight'
Stances (Dachi)	Kiba
Connections	The tekki kata are shorei kata, emphasizing strong, powerful techniques. These kata were revised or created by Yasutsune Itosu. Funakoshi was required to spend three years learning each tekki kata. Tekki Shodan was originally called Naihanchi and was revised by Itosu.
Synopsis	One of three kata originally thought to be training kata but a closer inspection will reveal a deeper cause. Defending on long boats or modern adaptation alleys, car parks, corridors. Also a training kata used to develop strong ligaments around the joints of the legs.
Number of Movements	29 Movements
Relevant Facts	The embusen of Tekki Katas is a straight line with the use of Kiba Dachi (Horse Straddle Stance throughout) There are 29 movements in tekki Shodan. Always starting and ending with a Rei (Bow)

The Advanced Shotokan Kata Manual

Visualise
Yoi

Technique 1
Tekki Shodan Yoi — Halfway — Haito Uke

Technique 5
Kage Zuki

Technique 6
Halfway

Technique 7
Mae Geri / Fumi Komi

Technique 11
Name Ashi

Technique 12
Sokumen Uke — Halfway

Technique 13
Nami Ashi

Tekki Shodan

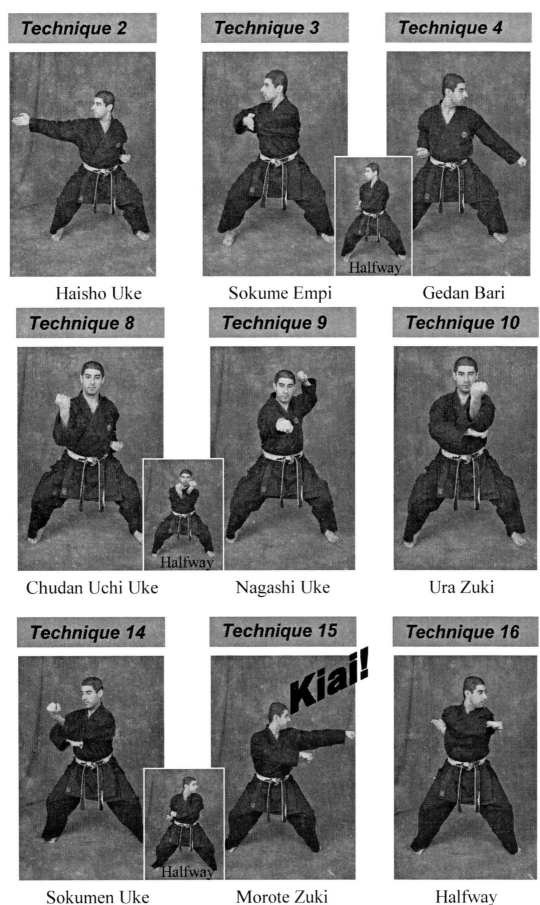

The Advanced Shotokan Kata Manual

Technique 17
Haisho Uke

Technique 18
Mawashi Empi

Technique 19
Sokumen Empi Uchi

Technique 23
Chudan Uchi Uke (Halfway)

Technique 24
Nagashi Uke

Technique 25
Ura Zuki

Technique 29
Morote Zuki (Halfway) — Kiai!

Finish
Tekki Sho-

Tekki Shodan

There are also benefits to performing Tekki katas in karate demonstrations…. Firstly they are the only kata that allow you to keep constant eye contact with the public. Secondly for training you can very easily correct yourself by performing them in front of a mirror.

They are incredibly hard to perform! Don't take them for granted…..

The Advanced Shotokan Kata Manual

Fumi Komi - Mika Zuki Geri

Tekki Shodan

Tekki Shodan - very rarely performed for gradings or in competition.

Senior Japanese teachers understood the importance of this kata and once the student spends some time studying it the true value will become clear!

Promoting strong ligament and lower body development they help increase physical strength without the need for weight training which probably did not exist at that time.

Modern application of course for this kata is fighting in alleyways, narrow streets, car parks (between two cars). In ancient days the application would have been Japanese boats - the dark streets of Tokoyo and the poorly lit roads of Okinawa travelling from one village to another!

'There are perhaps 100 kata across the various forms of karate, each with many minor variations. The number 108 is significant in Buddhism, and kata with 54, 36, or 27 moves (divisors of 108) are common'

Pictured Left: Two alleyways in modern Tokyo. The value of Tekki katas for these types of terrain are obvious.

Tekki Nidan

鉄騎二段

Name of Kata 'Iron Horse or Iron Knight'

Stances (Dachi) Kiba

Connections The tekki kata are shorei kata, emphasizing strong, powerful techniques. These kata were revised or created by Yasutsune Itosu. Funakoshi was required to spend three years learning each tekki kata. Tekki Shodan was originally called Naihanchi and was revised by Itosu.

Synopsis One of three kata originally thought to be training kata but a closer inspection will reveal a deeper cause. Defending on long boats or modern adaptation alleys, car parks, corridors.
Also a training kata used to develop strong ligaments around the joints of the legs.

Number of Movements 26 Movements

Relevant Facts The embusen of Tekki Katas is a straight line with the use of Kiba Dachi (Horse Straddle Stance throughout)

There are 29 movements in Tekki Shodan. Always starting and ending with a Rei (Bow)

The Advanced Shotokan Kata Manual

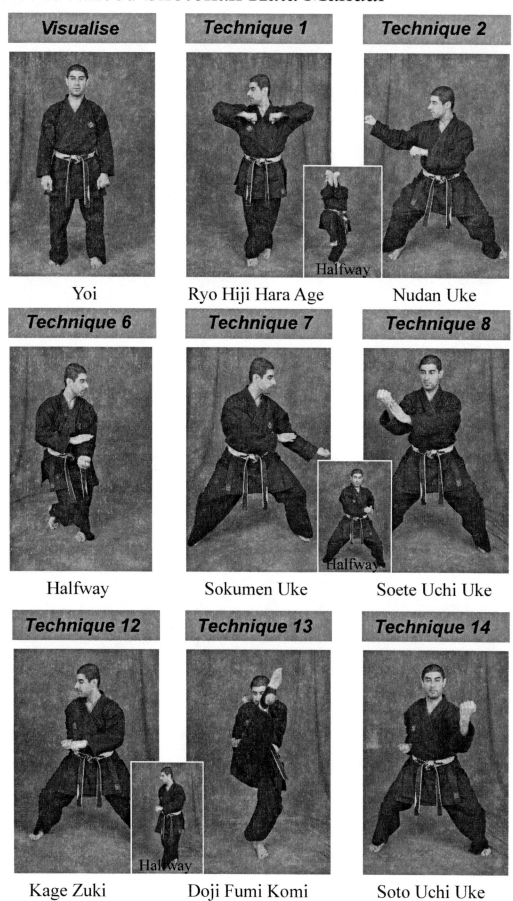

Tekki Nidan

Technique 3	Technique 4	Technique 5
Sokumen Uke	Ryo Hiji Hara Age	Nudan Uke

Technique 9	Technique 10	Technique 11

Doji Fumi Komi	Soete Mai Empi	Chudan Tate Shuto

Technique 15	Technique 16	Technique 17

Kosa Uke	Nagashi Uke	Jodan Ura Zuki

The Advanced Shotokan Kata Manual

Tekki Nidan is deceptively complicated! It is shorter than the other two kata in the series but the quick intricate hand movements between the Sokumen Uchi Uke and Doji Fumi Komi as above makes it extremely difficult. But very enjoyable!

Hard to believe that ordinary people can create such lovely techniques with so much thought an imagination!

'Imagination'….. It's the first thing we start to lose as we grow older!

Tekki Nidan

Technique 21 — Kage Zuki

Technique 22 — Doji Fumi komi (Halfway)

Technique 23 — Soto Uchi Uke

Karate was a working class art - i.e. before its introduction to universities it was practiced by farmers and local people who just wanted to learn to defend themselves and their crops.

Today after all this time some educational establishments do not see the real benefits to the 'hidden' values of the art.

Kata manages aggression, improves concentration and develops discipline. These values are not just principles but really attainable through training.

'No one saves us but ourselves.
No one can and no one may
We ourselves must walk the path'

Pictured Left: Japanese long boats used for fishing. Another option and idea for Tekki Katas. The side to side movement fits this type of defending

Tekki Sandan

鉄騎三段

Name of Kata	'Iron Horse - Iron Knight'
Stances (Dachi)	Kiba
Connections	Master Itosu is reported to have learned the kata from Sokon Matsumura, who learned it from a Chinese man living in Tomari. Itosu is thought to have changed the original kata. Naihanchi would traditionally be taught first in Tomari-te and Shuri-te schools, which indicates its importance. Gichin Funakoshi learned the kata from Anko Asato. Funakoshi renamed the kata Tekki (Iron Horse) in reference to his old teacher, Itosu, and the form's power.
Synopsis	The code **1-7-8-1-6-4-6** is a relevant timing application used by senior grades to perform this kata. Pausing for split seconds between techniques and slightly longer pauses between the above count.
Number of movements	34 Movements
Relevant Facts	The side to side movements in a low stance build up the necessary balance and strength for fast footwork and body shifting. Naihanchi/Tekki, the result is the Hachi-monji, or figure eight stance. This has been called the basics of all karate

Tekki Sandan

Technique 3
Technique 4
Technique 5

Ude Hasami
(Left hand Position - Zenwan- Munue-Mae- Suihei- Kamae)

Ura Zuki

Halfway

Technique 1
Technique 2

Gedan Oishi Uke

Disengage

Tettsui Uchi

Technique 8
Technique 1

Jodan Ura Zuki

Halfway

Soto Uchi Uke

The Advanced Shotokan Kata Manual

Ude Hasami   Ura Zuki   Chudan Zuki
(Left Hand Position - Zenwan Chudan Uke)

Ken Chudan Choko Zuki   Tate Shuto Uke   Kage Zuki

Nagashi Uke   Jodan Ura Zuki   Yame

Tekki Sandan

A good training game to develop strong stances for this kata is to start a Sumo competition without the throwing.

Begin with a big circle and ask the students to enter the centre one at a time with the winner staying in the circle until there is no one else to beat! They have fun and you develop their Kiba Dachi! Everyone wins!

The Advanced Shotokan Kata Manual

Beautiful circular movements
help create momentum and power

Tekki Sandan

'The hardest of the three Tekki Kata. Eye and hand coordination are tested to their fullest and the movements once again strengthen the knee ligaments and quadriceps.

The heavy work rate of the arms also develops the biceps and triceps muscles! The count **1,7,8 1,6,4,6** helps create equilibrium in the execution of the form. Giving the entire kata structure rather than a continuous running programme!'

It is also ironic that as the body is constantly fighting the mind; this Kata helps create order and balance! Study it and you will see'

The future in Safe Hands

Top Right: Lotti in deep concentration!
Bottom Left: Tilly 'Grand Champion'
Centre Right: Georgia focused!

The Advanced Shotokan Kata Manual

What is Kata ?

Kata is professional. It starts and finishes with a bow. It is performed in a set manner with no deviations and requires the highest level of concentration. It is impossible to perfect and the more you work at it the harder it becomes. Just like a relationship it blossoms with age!

Kata knows your mind. It knows all of your weaknesses, strengths, fears and understands how to get the best out of.

It is demanding in its relationship with you. It requires constant mental and physical attention and dictates the rules. It is in charge and not you! The worries of modern day living can be left behind but you are playing the game according to its rules. You need room for it and time.

It's a perfect match. Unlike most sports which require teamwork. Kata is the one activity which can be performed in a group but ultimately it is about the individual. It is a personal journey. Hopefully a pleasant one. It is a form of meditation without the need to learn how to meditate. The more you engross yourself in the kata the deeper the trance becomes. It is emotional in that it requires 100% commitment which is exhausting.

Kata will stay true to you and in return only requires you show it respect, loyalty, and patience…..perhaps Kata is about perfecting you're life for a split second before returning to a state of imperfection which is the human condition!

Surely it is the pursuit of that perfection which drives us all in this worthwhile cause. As long as we realise it will never be truly reached.

The Advanced Shotokan Kata Manual Grading System

Traditional Shotokan Grades

Belt Color	Japanese	Training period between grades
White	Ungraded	N/a
Blue	10th Kyu	3 mths
Red	9th Kyu	3 mnhs
Orange	8th Kyu	3 mths
Yellow	7th Kyu	3 mths
Green	6th Kyu	3 mhs
Purple	5th Kyu	3 mths
Purple/White	4th Kyu	3 mths
Brown	3rd Kyu	3 mths
Brown / White	2nd Kyu	3 mths
Brown / Red	1st Kyu	6 mths
1st Dan	Shodan	1 yr
2nd Dan	Nidan	2 yrs
3rd Dan	Sandan	3 yrs
4th Dan	Yondan	4 yrs
5th dan	Godan	5 yrs
6th Dan	Rokudan	6 yrs
7th Dan	Nanadan	7 yrs
8th Dan	Hachidan	8 yrs
9th Dan	Kudan	9 yrs
10th Dan	Judan	10 yrs

10 Kyu Grades - Junior grades   **10 Dan grades** - Senior grades

Grading System

GRADING REQUIREMENTS	CONTENT	EXPLANATION
Mental	Physical and emotional strength	Lead up and during grading!(Tell tale signs)
Etiquette	Start & end with a Bow	This should be second nature by now
Technique	Understand outline & direction of kata	Working knowledge of kata, basically knows it
Stances	Forward, Back, Horse Straddle Stance etc.	Stances are identifiable by the examiner
Advanced Skill Sets	Correct timing, distancing, & judgement in kata	Slow techniques are slow and fast are executed fast
Discretionary Factors	Age Character Training Attendance	Maturity of student Confidence Levels Regular or not what were the factors? Sickness, holiday etc.
	Individual disabilities & Limitations	Mental or physical
Administrative	Student holds a valid License	Student responsibility
	Grading fee	Student responsibility
	Student has informed his/her instructor wishes to take grading exam	A positive decision to take the exam. Not pushed into it!

The Advanced Shotokan Kata Manual

We use the following ranking system for Shotokan Karate. Please bear in mind Kihon (Basics) and Kumite (Sparring) are separate exams and form part of the overall assessment for the grade sought:

- ### **BROWN BELT - 3RD KYU**
  The following kata:

  Tekki Shodan - plus any previous kata from the choice of the following:

  Taikayoku Shodan - Heian Shodan - Heian Nidan
  Heian Sandan - Heian Yondan - Heian Godan

- ### **BROWN / WHITE STRIPE - 2ND KYU**
  One kata of your choice from the following:

  Bassai Dai - Kanku Dai - Enpi - Jion - plus any previous kata from the choice of the following:

  Taikayoku Shodan - Heian Shodan - Heian Nidan
  Heian Sandan - Heian Yondan - Heian Godan

- ### **BROWN / RED STRIPE - 1ST KYU**
  One kata of your choice from the following (please note the same kata cannot be chosen if performed for a previous grade):

  Bassai Dai - Kanku Dai - Enpi - Jion - plus any previous kata from the choice of the following:

  Taikayoku Shodan - Heian Shodan - Heian Nidan
  Heian Sandan - Heian Yondan - Heian Godan

Grading System

CONSIDERATIONS: Eye direction, concentration, stance, posture, timing, distance, accelaration, kiai, speed, breathing, feeling settled and external actions

- **SHODAN - 1ST DAN**

    One kata of your choice from the following. The candidate may be asked to explain meaning of selected katas. (please note the same kata cannot be chosen if performed for a previous grade):

    Bassai Dai - Kanku Dai - Enpi - Jion

    plus any previous kata from the choice of the following:

    Taikayoku Shodan - Heian Shodan - Heian Nidan
    Heian Sandan - Heian Yondan - Heian Godan

- **NIDAN - 2ND DAN**

    One kata of your choice from the following. The candidate may be asked to explain meaning of selected katas. (please note the same kata cannot be chosen if performed for a previous grade):

    Bassai Dai - Jion - Enpi - Kanku Dai - Hangetsu - Jitte
    Gankaku - Tekki Nidan - Tekki Sandan - Nijushiho

    One of the following of the examiners choice:

    Bassai Dai - Jion - Enpi - Kanku Dai

Please note:

The karate practitioner is ultimately the person responsible for making the decision on whether to grade or not. Your instructor can provide feedback and can even sometimes encourage you to take a grading. Encouragement has to be measured and realistic.

The Advanced Shotokan Kata Manual

- ### **SANDAN - 3RD DAN**
  One kata of your choice from the following:

  Bassai Dai - Jion - Empi - Kanku Dai - Hangetsu - Jitte
  Gankaku - Tekki Nidan - Tekki Sandan - Sochin

  One of the following of the examiners choice:

  Bassai Dai - Jion - Enpi - Kanku Dai

- ### **YONDAN - 4TH DAN**
  Any Kata of the examiners choice (from the previous exams) including the following:

  Unsu - Gojushiho Dai - Gojushiho Sho

  Plus the demonstration of teaching ability by the candidate for the selected kata. Explaining bunkai (applications) for the kata to demonstrate higher understanding.

- ### **GODAN - 5TH DAN**
  Be prepared to perform any kata in the Shotokan system although most common practice is to still ask your choice.

In certain styles, *shodan* implies that all the basics of the style have been mastered. At **sandan** the student is deemed capable of teaching independently as a teacher or instructor, often called sensei. At *Godan,* the *budōka* may receive certification as a master level practitioner **(Shidōin).** Generally, the lower dan ranks are validated on the basis of knowledge and physical skill. The higher the dan rank, the more leadership ability, teaching experience, and service to the style play a role in promotion.

The Karate Gi

The karate gi appears to have been developed from the Judo uniform. When Gichin Funakoshi demonstrated karate in Japan at the *Kodokan*, (Judo headquarters).

Different styles of Karate have slightly different uniforms though all share the same basic design, differing only in the lengths of sleeves, legs and the skirt of the uwagi (jacket). Many karateka tend to wear their obi (belt) much longer than judoka and other martial artists. Ultimately its what is under the Gi that is of importance!
The mindset and faithfulness to Karate-Do!

The Advanced Shotokan Kata Manual

Mia Matous with spirit!

If you are under the impression that women lack the physical strength or skill to perform Karate just attend any championship today or advanced training class.

Even in today's forward thinking society, a woman starting in any martial arts training program is often subjected to many responses from friends, and often family,. These responses are based upon misinformation. Karate does not make women aggressive just as it does not make them less attractive! It builds confidence and keeps the body firm!

Karate benefits everyone and today more women / girls practice it than the traditional male dominated art of old.

Their spirit and approach to techniques is calculated and especially with Kata! The speed and precision of performing is just as good as the men.

If we put a limitation on who can and cannot practice karate we are selling the martial arts short!

Julia Pell, a wife, mother, & martial artist

Top Left - Julia Pell performing Hiza Geri
Top right - Mia Matous ready for battle!
Bottom Left - Denise Kenny - Kyokushin Kan
Bottom Right - Stavroula Kontostathi - The Way!

Samurai (侍 or sometimes 士) is a common term for a warrior in pre-industrial Japan. A more appropriate term is bushi (武士) (lit. "war-man") which came into use during the Edo period. However, the term samurai now usually refers to warrior nobility, not, for example, ashigaru or foot soldiers. The samurai with no attachment to a clan or daimyo was called a ronin (lit. "wave-man").

The 47 Ronin - A Story Of Honor

The story of the 47 Ronin is one of the most celebrated in the history of the samurai. This was perhaps all the more so because it occurred at a time when the samurai class was struggling to maintain a sense of itself - warriors with no war, a social class without a function.

The tale could be said to have begun with the teachings of Yamaga Soko (1622-1685), an influential theorist. His writings inspired a certain Ôishi Kuranosuke Yoshio, a samurai and retainer of Asano Takumi no kami Naganori (1667-1701), who led a branch of the powerful Asano family.

It happened that Lord Asano was chosen by the shogun, Tokugawa Tsunayoshi, to be one of a number of daimyo tasked with entertaining envoys from the Imperial family. To assist him in this new duty, the Bakufu's highest ranking master of protocol, Kira Kozukenosuke Yoshinaka (1641-1702), was assigned to instruct him in matters of etiquette. Kira, it seems, was a somewhat difficult character and expected Asano to compensate him monetarily for the trouble, which Asano held was simply his duty. The two grew to dislike one another intensely, and Kira made every effort to embarrass his student. Finally, in April of 1702, the situation exploded within the shogun's palace - Kira insulted Asano once again, prompting the latter to draw his sword and swing at him. Kira was only wounded in the attack and Asano was promptly placed under confinement.

Striking another man in anger was against the law - doing so within the shogun's palace was unthinkable. Asano made little effort to defend himself during questioning except to say that he bore the shogun no ill will and only regretted that he had failed to kill Kira.

The Shogunate passed down a sentence of death on Asano, ordering him to slit his belly at once. The shogun also decreed that his 50,000-koku fief at Akô in Harima was to be confiscated and his brother Daigaku placed under house arrest. When the news of the unfortunate event reached Asano's castle, his retainers were thrown into an uproar

The Advanced Shotokan Kata Manual

and argued heatedly over what to do next. Some favored accepting their lot quietly and dispersing as 'Ronin', while another group called for a defense of the castle and an actual battle with the government. Ôishi Kuranosuke, who urged the retainers to give up the castle peacefully and struggle to rehabilitate the Asano family while at the same time preparing to take revenge on Kira, sounded the view that prevailed.

Accordingly, a band of Asano retainers - now ronin - set out on a carefully planned road to revenge. Kira was no fool, and expecting some sort of attempt on his life by the Asano men increased his personal guard. To this end the ronin hid away a cache of weapons and armor before ostensibly dispersing, some taking up menial jobs while others, Ôishi left his wife and began frequenting all of Edo's houses of ill repute, carousing with prostitutes and engaging in drunken brawls. On one occasion, a samurai from Satsuma is supposed to have come across Ôishi drunk in the street and spat upon him, saying that he was no real samurai.

Needless to say, Kira began to doubt that he was in any real danger, and had relaxed his guard. It was at that point that the ronin struck. 47 of them gathered on 14 December 1702 and, after donning the armor and taking up the weapons from the cache, they set out on their revenge on that same snowy night. They divided into two groups and attacked, with one group entering through the rear of the compound while the rest forced their way through the front, battering the gate down with a mallet. Kira's men, many of whom were killed or wounded, were taken completely by surprise but did put up a spirited resistance (one of the ronin was killed in the attack), though ultimately to no avail: Kira was found in an outhouse and presented to Ôishi, who offered him the chance to commit suicide. When Kira made no reply, Ôishi struck off his head with the same dagger that Asano had used to kill himself with. They turned themselves in.

The 47 Ronin - A Story Of Honor

Grave of the 47 ronin, Sengakuji temple

The assassination of Kira placed the government in a difficult situation. After all, the 46 survivors now awaiting their fate had lived up to the standards of loyalty expected of true samurai and the ideals propounded by such men as Yamaga Soko. Additionally, the decision to order Asano to commit suicide and confiscate his domain while taking no action against Kira had not been popular Nonetheless, the Bakufu decided that the maintenance of order would once again have to prevail, and so the ronin were ordered to commit suicide - a sentence suggested by the famous Confucian scholar Ogyû Sorai (1666-1728). They were at this time divided up into four groups under guard by four different daimyo, yet once they had all died, their bodies were buried together at the Sengakuji. Legend has it that the Satsuma samurai who had spit upon Ôishi in the street came to the temple and slit his own belly to atone for his insults.

1. Karate-do begins with courtesy and ends with rei.
2. There is no first strike in karate.
3. Karate is an aid to justice.
4. First know yourself before attempting to know others.
5. Spirit first, technique second.
6. Always be ready to release your mind.
7. Accidents arise from negligence.
8. Do not think that karate training is only in the dojo.
9. It will take your entire life to learn karate, there is no limit.
10. Put your everyday living into karate and you will find "Myo" (subtle secrets).
11. Karate is like boiling water, if you do not heat it constantly, it will cool.
12. Do not think that you have to win, think rather that you do not have to lose.
13. Victory depends on your ability to distinguish vulnerable points from invulnerable ones.
14. The out come of the battle depends on how you handle weakness and strength.
15. Think of your opponents hands and feet as swords.
16. When you leave home, think that you have numerous opponents waiting for you.
17. Beginners must master low stance and posture, natural body positions are for the advanced.
18. Practicing a kata exactly is one thing, engaging in a real fight is another.
19. Do not forget to correctly apply: strength and weakness of power, stretching and contraction of the body, and slowness
20. Always think and devise ways to live the precepts of karate-do every day.

Ancient masters

Seisho Arakaki

Tode Sakugawa

Bushi Matsumura

Kanryo Higashionna

Modern Karate

Itosu Yasutsune

Gichin Funakoshi

After World War II

Masatoshi Nakayama

Gogen Yamaguch

Oyama Masutatsu

The Advanced Shotokan Kata Manual

The Development of Modern day karate

Okinawa karate developed during XVII and XVIII century. There are very few written testimonies and we have to base this on oral tradition. Earliest stories remembers masters such as: "Chinese fist" Sakugawa, Kushanku and Yara from Chatan. All of them lived during XVIII century. In XIX century, most famous masters were: Matsumura the Warrior and Higashonna the Lion. During this period karate was practiced in secrecy, individually, from master to teacher. Persons who learned karate were almost all court officials or have had family relations to Shuri court. Old karate was practiced exclusively as method of self-defense, each master knew only one or few katas and each kata was self-standing method of self-defense. They all had an opportunity to travel to Fuchow (China) and to learn chuan fa methods.

Modern karate was developed by master Itosu. Itosu learned karate from Matsumura. His goal was to remove shadow of secrecy and to include karate into Okinawa schools. Therefore, he changed karate. He promoted kata as suitable method of practice, since it was safe and appropriate for class. All dangerous techniques were modified (eye poke, groin kick, throat strike...) so that school children can practice safely. Itosu devised Pinan katas also referred to as Heian, combining modified parts of old karate katas.

The Chinese Description o f the Tiger

Tigers may not be the king of the jungle, but these striped cats are no softies! Magnetic and self-possessed, Tigers are born leaders. They have an air of authority that prompts others to fall in line, which is exactly how they like it. Although they are magnetically charming and fun to be around, Tigers like to go it alone sometimes too. A Tiger's main interest is in following its ambitions -- and maintaining control.

Tigers are courageous beyond compare and generally come out ahead in battle. Seduction is one area where the Tiger is definitely king! Noble and warm-hearted, Tigers have a natural, raw appeal that's extremely attractive. They're not just about attraction, though; ever on the side of right, Tigers will fight the good fight to the bitter end if the cause is worthy. Opponents are wise to fear this feline.

They seldom attack unless forced into a corner. But from that corner they will defend their honor to the death!

A bit of caution is a good thing around Tigers, since they can pounce without warning. They experience mood swings and often feel things more intensely than others, the latter quality being both good and bad. They can react poorly under stress and are prone to emotional outbursts. This Sign's bristling sensitivity can send friend and foe running for cover.

A lesson that Tigers would be well-served to learn is moderation in all things. Once these cats can find their center and direct their considerable energies toward worthwhile endeavors.

Maybe Shotokan ironically has more in common with the tiger than we thought!

Frank loves to meet new people and spread his message and you can help him do that!

Yoi - Getting Ready

This position is more than just about the physical act of getting ready. It also signifies the mental act of being alert, on guard, and prepared. I think about the Kata, the masters who created them… it's an honor to be able to practice them! Everything in karate is in kata and it starts from this position!

The Advanced Shotokan Kata Manual

A
Age: Lift up (Rising technique)
Age-Uke: (Jodan-uke): Upper block
Age-zuki: Upward punch
Ate-waza: Hitting techniques

B

C
Choku: Straight
Chudan: Middle
Chudan-choku-zuki: Middle straight punch
Chudan-shuto-uke: Middle knife-hand block

D
Dachi: Stance
Dojo: Gym, training hall. Literally 'Way Place'

E
Empi: Elbow
Empi uchi: Elbow strike

F
Fudo-dachi: Inverted parallel stance
Fumikomi: Downward (stomping) kick

G
Gedan: Low
Gedan-kekomi: Low thrust kick
Gedan-zuki: Low punch
Gedan-Uke: Low block
Gi: Karate Uniform
Gyaku-zuki: Reverse punch

Glossary

H
Hachiji-dachi: Natural stance (hip width 45 foot angle)
Haishu: Back hand (open hand)
Haishu uchi: Back hand strike
Haishu uke: Back hand block
Haisoku: Upper part of foot
Haito: Ridge hand
Haito uchi: Ridgehand strike
Hajime: Begin or start (command given ofr sparring competition)
Hangetsu-dachi: Half-moon Stance
Hanmi: Forward Stance with hip at 45
Heiko-dachi: Parallel stance
Heisoku-dachi: Informal attention stance
Hidari: Left
Hiji: Elbow
Hiji-ate: Elbow strike
Hiji-uchi: Elbow strike
Hiraken: Hand technique where the fingers are bent at the first finger joint
Hittsui: Knee
Hizagashira: Knee cap

I

J
Ju-Kumite: Free Sparring
Jodan: Upper
Jodan-age-uke: Upper/upward block
Jodan-choku-zuki: High straight punch
Jodan-kekomi: High thrust kick
Jodan-mae-geri: High front kick
Juji-uke: Cross hand blockand

The Advanced Shotokan Kata Manual

K
Kagi-zuki: Hook punch
Kaisho: Open hand
Kakuto: Heel
Karate: Empty Hand
Kata: Form (Sequence or movement)
Keage: Snap Kick
Kekomi: Thrust Kick
Kentsui: Outside edge of the hand when clenched
Keri (Geri): Kick
Keri-waza: Kicking technique
Kiba-dachi: Horse stance
Kihon-Kumite: Basic Sparring
Kizami-zuki: Jab
Kokutsu-dachi: Back stance (70 weight on the back leg, 30 on the front)
Ko-Shi: Ball of the foot
Kumite: Sparring

L
M
Mae-ashi-geri: Kick with the front leg
Mae-empi-uchi: Front elbow strike
Mae-geri: Front kick
Mae-geri-keage: Front snap kick
Mae-hiji-ate: Forward elbow strike
Makiwara: A board rooted in the ground used to hit to practice focus
Mawashi-geri: Roundhouse kick
Mawashi-zuki: Roundhouse punch
Migi: Right
Mikazuki-geri: Crescent kick (Kick with the inside of the foot)
Modotte: Command to return to original spot or posture.

Glossary

N
Nai-wan: Nami-ashi-geri: Crecent kick (block) Neko-ashi-dachi:
Nukite: knife hand strike (palm flat, strike with finger tips)

O
O-Sensei: Founding sensei of the style (Tsuyoshi Chitose for Chito Ryu Karate)
O-Uchi Mawashi geri: Roundhoouse kick (From back leg)

P Q

R
Rei: Bow Ren zuki: Continuous punches Rohai: Kata Name Ryote: Double (strike or block) Ryu San: Kata Name Rinten: Full turn (techniques involving a turn of 360°)

S
Seiza: Sit (command)
San Shin: Kata Name
Shi Ho Hai: Kata Name
San Shi Riu: Kata Name
Seisan: Kata Name
Soto (uke): Outside (block)
Sukui Uke: Scooping block
Sayuzuki: Double strike (usually in shiko dachi)

T
Tai sabaki: body movement (evasive techniques)
Tettsui uchi: Strike with bottom of closed fist (aka kensui uchi)
Tenshin: Kata Name
Te-Hodoki: Hand release techniques
Te: Hand (kara-TE = empty hand)
Tsuki: punch (aka Zuki)
Tanden: Lower abdomen, seat of Ki or Chi
Temeshiwara: Breaking techniques

The Advanced Shotokan Kata Manual

U
Uke: Block
Ura: Upside down or inverted

V W X

Y
Yoko: Side Yame: Stop (command)
Yoi: Begin (command)
Yama Zuki: Y-Block (one hand down, one hand over head)

Z
Zuki: punch (aka Tsuki)